Miniature Wood Carvings of Africa

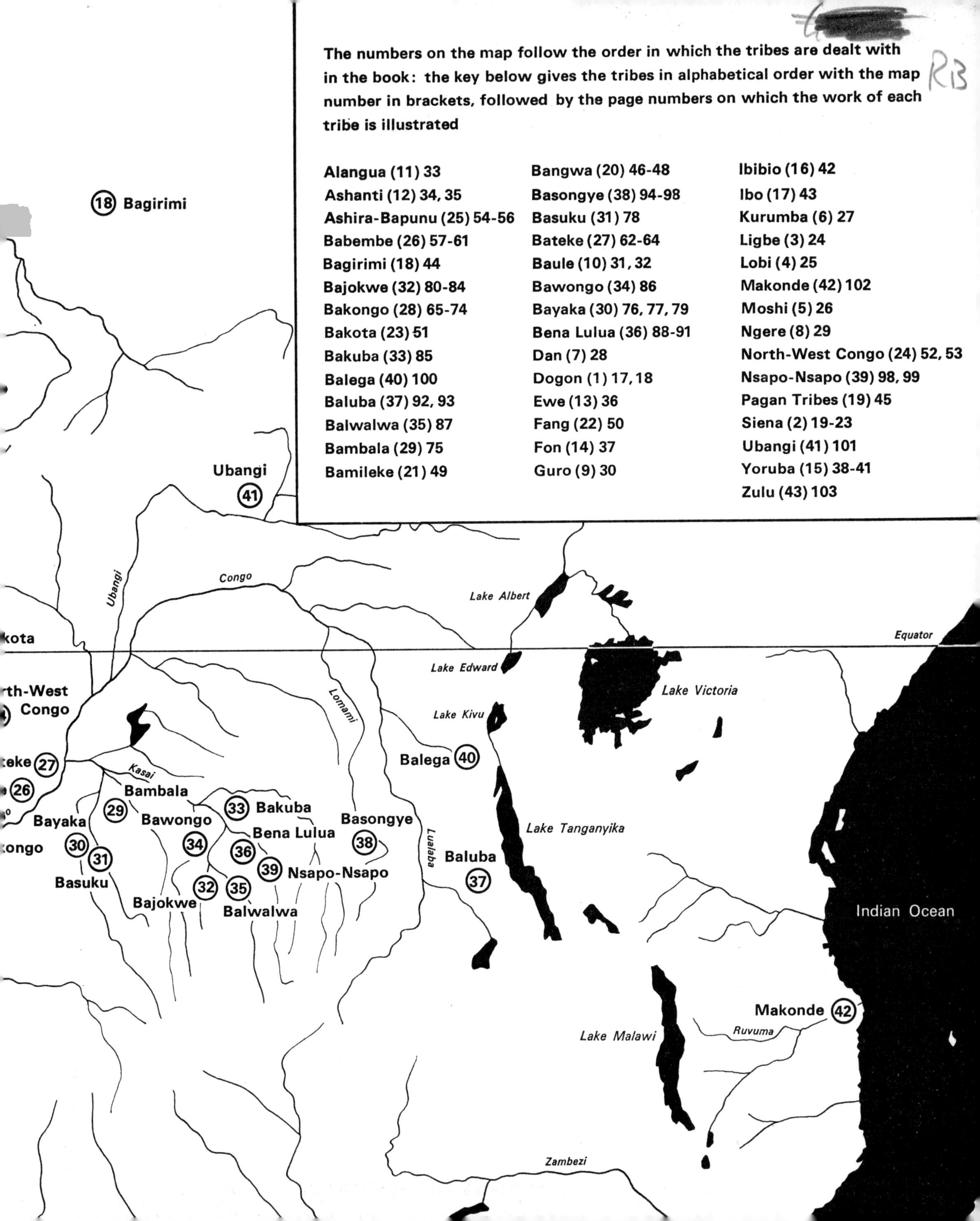

The numbers on the map follow the order in which the tribes are dealt with in the book: the key below gives the tribes in alphabetical order with the map number in brackets, followed by the page numbers on which the work of each tribe is illustrated

Miniature Wood Carvings of Africa

William Fagg

with a foreword by Josef Herman

First published in 1970 by Adams & Dart
40 Gay Street, Bath, and in the USA by
New York Graphic Society, Greenwich, Connecticut

SBN 239 00018 8

Designed by Barry Robson
Photographs by R. A. Burn, Sudbury, Suffolk
Printed by Alfieri & Lacroix, Milan
Bound in Great Britain

Contents

Foreword

It may seem superfluous to single out of a tradition known for its homogeneity a group of works for no better reason than that they are small. However, something can be said for their unique place in African art and for their specific aesthetics. They are not 'small studies for bigger works'—this European habit is not shared by the tribal carvers—nor are they 'copies of larger works'. Whether made as fetishes or as decorative sections of objects of everyday use, or for purely aesthetic reasons as figurines in themselves, the quality can be equally high and as characteristic of the styles of African tribes as are the larger and better known works.

As for their aesthetics, we need only remind the reader of the physical fact that, just as a monumental form will gain in impact the larger the size, by the same token a form tends to be intimate, even endearing, when made on a small scale, and thus easy to handle. The very tactile quality will call out a different emotional response than do the larger objects we can only look at.

African miniatures are not limited to the charm of their minuteness. They can and often do convey the drastic power of a more expressive kind. It is amazing how big, in such cases, a small form can be! A half-inch head can be, and usually is, carved with great feeling for mass, volume and weight. Nor is the final form merely rudimentary, merely 'sketched'. The carver's sense of unity sees to it that all imaginative deliberations are kept within a well-defined outline. Absolute perfection within and even above the framework of its own culture is the ultimate achievement. No surface seems too small for the inclusion of the characteristics—more often stylised than 'represented'—of the tribal type: a complicated hairdress, scarifications on body and face, shape of eyes and all other features, etc. This is something other than a concession to 'naturalism'. It is the link between the abstract element and its source. More like the early Cubists' works when the formal inventions were echoes of objects (still-life), landscape and the human figure than the abstract developments which came with Mondrian and Malevitch. Of course this link between abstract inventiveness and its sources is also characteristic of the bigger tribal sculpture. But what is astonishing is that nothing is made 'easy' in the small scale, neither the formal complexity and care for essential detail, nor the bolder synthesis.

Miniature sculpture is not the prerogative of Africa. Other cultures whether of ancient Mexico or Egypt, India or Europe are well known for the seriousness with which they treated small works. It is my belief that African miniatures make a specific contribution to the arts of mankind and should be as known as the minute works of more celebrated cultures.

Finally, a word about the 'age' of the pieces and about patination in general, problems which seem to worry many people. It appears to me that in themselves neither is a guarantee of quality. The exact age in African art is often impossible to determine—besides, there are also 'old' pot-boilers—and patination, precisely because of its seductive quality, can easily distract from the more important quality of the form. Also, patina can be artificially induced or faked. Thus the real question is: how good is the piece of sculpture, does it work as art, has it conviction as well as feeling, has it the marks of creative energy, etc. I have it on good authority that 'some of the pieces in this book are probably as much as a century old, and that all are more or less of equal age'.

Having lived with some of these small works for well over twenty years my enthusiasm is not only for obvious masterly achievements but for the general quality of total sculpture the humblest of them seem to possess.

The author of the book, William Fagg, is of course the well-known and internationally respected writer of numerous books and articles on African Art, and the Keeper of the Department of Ethnography of the British Museum. It is to him as scholar and friend that I should like to extend my warmest thanks for his generosity and consideration.

Josef Herman

Introduction

I am happy that my friend Josef Herman, whose collection of African miniature forms the subject matter of this book, has agreed to my suggestion that he should write some account of his feelings about it, as the collector but above all as an artist. For I am not an artist—at least I surmise that if I were I should have dared to try my hand before this—and I see the truths of art as in a glass darkly, in humble imitation of my artist friends, if I see them at all. To many doctrinaire ethnologists and social anthropologists the attempt to do so will doubtless seem misguided and irrelevant; dedicated to the mistaken proposition that science can proceed only by inductive methods, they admit no use of the intuition and put all their faith in analysis. Many years ago, talking to my friend Leon Underwood, the sculptor and one of the most penetrating interpreters of African art, I incautiously said something about using ethnographical analysis to get nearer to the nature of a work of art. He replied, so far as I remember, that I should be very lucky if I succeeded, since every work of art is a synthesis. If we analysed this synthesis, we should find that—hey presto—the work of art had disappeared. It would seem that it is not what the artist makes it from, but what he makes it into that matters. (It occurs to me that much the same is true of humour, which has much in common with art; and the idea of academic persons solemnly applying analysis to art and humour suggests irresistibly to me a modern tale of the Wise Men of Gotham.)

The idea of art as synthesis is of course far from being a new one. It has been recognised in language from as far back as we can go—to our hypothetical mother-tongue Indo-European, in which philologists find a root $\sqrt{}$AR associated with the meaning of 'fitting together'; it is the source not only of 'art' but also of 'harmony' and a constellation of related terms. Perhaps in its most primitive form it described the first truly human act. And here we are reminded of another idea of the seer Underwood, the priority of tool form over art form.

To revert to ethnology—if, as is the case, most of the great advances in the natural sciences are made by intuitive leaps and not by induction alone, then surely ethnology, which is half science, half humanity, must *a fortiori* accept the full use of both parts of the human mind, intellect and intuition. As the comparative study of the cultures of peoples, should it not be the most all-embracing of disciplines? Can it exclude a great part of human experience and achievement on the ground that it can only be known by the eye of faith? But if ethnology, in order to do its work properly, must admit the subjective as well as the objective judgement, then art studies and art history, when they are applied to the arts of tribal society, have need of the help of objective ethnology or anthropology if they are not to be led astray. For example, Western artists may know intuitively that they share with the tribal artists certain universal values in art, and they may well be led to suppose that such a partial community of thought between Europeans and Africans must be found in very much greater measure between Africans of one tribe and Africans of another; yet this is not generally so. A 'blockage' seems to occur, deriving from the exclusivity of the tribal system, which inhibits a man (or did so while the system was fully effective) from appreciating or taking cognisance of sculptures beyond the writ of his tribal language and religion.

This is by no means to say that the tribal Africans, before their culture was affected by European influences, had an inferior mental equipment to ours for the critical appreciation of works of art; rather, they were in the happy position of not yet having separated art and belief, as we have done only in the last two centuries or so. Consequently, when confronted by an image used in an alien religion, and made in a correspondingly alien style, their rejection of it as something outlandish on religious grounds left them with no *separate* set of canons by which to evaluate it as a 'pure' work of art. Of course, this short account somewhat oversimplifies the case, and a skilled carver of one tribe would not be unaware of the problems met by a carver of another tribe and how he had solved them; we must remember too, that tribes are not static entities delineated by rigid lines on a map, but are constantly changing by fission or fusion (a process to which the nearest parallels are to be found in cytology); but broadly speaking, barriers such as I have described do appear to have played a great part in enabling Africa to develop thousands of separate styles during the same period when Europe was developing one.

It would be well if the disciplines of learning in the West were to adopt a much more dynamic attitude (in sympathy, perhaps, with the dynamically evolving tribes of Africa) towards the boundaries between them. Too few people have time or inclination for concern about the galloping progress of the fragmentation of the sciences, which has advanced far from the days when 'polymath' was a highly respectable term. Almost invariably the development is in the direction of fission of disciplines, not of fusion. We should seek fields in which the tide may be reversed, and one of these is undoubtedly African art, in which ethnologist and artist are beginning to feel that they cannot do without each other if they are to make progress. Let us by all means encourage the breaking-down of the remaining barriers of mutual contempt which still exists on the official, theoretical plane, and foster the growth of a unified study of African art—or, since we must not be guilty of sowing the seeds of an African isolationism, of tribal art, for the same discipline is needed in all parts of the world where non-literate or pre-industrial peoples practise art. Indeed, in this sense—in which it is a necessary adjunct to the use of Europe-based study techniques on tribal peoples—anthropology is well called the science of cultural translation.

Museum ethnologists have in practice, and often without admitting it even to themselves, from the beginning adopted a middle ground between art and science, in the course of developing an empirical acquisition policy, and also of answering enquiries from the public. Indeed, value judgements, which are supposed to belong to art rather than to science, tend increasingly to dominate the attitudes of curators, and the more so those of the best curators, as they gain experience. The distinction of genuine pieces from forgeries and of good pieces from bad or mediocre ones, and the appraisal in monetary terms of pieces offered to the museum—all these call for the play of aesthetic or artistic judgement. (The tribal identification of a piece may be in part an aesthetic judgement, but is not necessarily so.)

Our practising ethnologist, if he has within him the capacity for improvement, or, much more rarely, a little of the divine spark, is likely sooner or later to develop the ability of instantaneous appreciation, so that in most cases his critical judgement is arrived at with certainty and in a flash, though he may then proceed to bolster it at leisure by rational argument. To undergo this process in oneself tends to confirm one's view of the absolute inexplicability of the intuition and its works—or so I thought for many years until recently. But I am now inclined to think that it may be seen in a more rational light as two near-simultaneous processes: first, the instantaneous recognition that the artist has succeeded (or, as the case maybe, has failed) in the task which he has set himself; and secondly, the further recognition that this task is an artistic one, either within the terms of his own culture or in absolute terms, or is not so. It is possible for instance, to realise that a carver for the tourist trade has performed superlatively well the task of producing a photographic likeness of his subject, and at the same time to recognise that that task is not art, whether considered in universal terms or, still less, in those of his own culture. For *tribal* Africans, though they do not verbalise the concept of art as we do, nevertheless have a much clearer idea of what is *not* art than does the ordinary Western civilised man, who is typically confused on this subject—no doubt precisely because of Western verbalisations about art. (In fact, this confusion, aided by the insidious attractions of naturalistic magazine and other illustrations, is the spearhead of cultural detribalisation.) But when one is faced with a fine work of tribal art, one first rejoices with the sculptor that he has triumphantly solved the problem or problems in sculpture presented by the work (noting for example how he has introduced regularities not present in nature by enlarging one feature, reducing another, eliminating a third), and then goes on to realise not only that his success is in the truest sense an artistic success, but that he has, so to speak, fully liberated his subject (as distinct from his mere subject *matter*) from the mute wood block, where a lesser artist might have left it obscure and 'blind'.

Form without subject (says Underwood) is the malaise of modern Western art. The tribal artist has, of course, never learnt to question the unity of form and subject; when he does he will no longer be tribal. It is ironical that when the European revolutionary painters about the turn of the century 'discovered' tribal art, they used it largely as a lever to overthrow the existing order of things in art and to substitute one in which, among other things, form would be an end in itself. Gradually some of the better modern artists began to see something less destructive in tribal art.

In Picasso's case—though he often amuses himself by denying any influence from Negro art—actual 'quotations' of pieces in his collection are often evident in his own works, though no doubt influences arising from his deep study of form are also less superficially embedded. Epstein, who amassed the greatest of all collections of tribal art, often expressed his admiration for his African or Melanesian masterpieces in a way that has nothing whatever in common with plagiarism (to accusations of which by little minds he was perenially subject): the brilliant originality of the angle of the head of *Lazarus* is not in the least diminished by the fact that it may be connected with the head of a child on his mother's back in an Idoma figure from Nigeria; the great *Venus* series is inseparably linked with what was perhaps the sculptor's favourite African work, a Fang 'Venus' (as he lovingly called it), but his use of the African work was entirely transmuted to his own artistic purpose.

Josef Herman's collection of miniatures (supplemented in his house by a number of excellent large sculptures) is one of the best specialised collections known to me. It is most admirably chosen as to both authenticity and quality. The miniatures are unpretentious by their nature, yet many of them can stand on equal terms with other pieces from the same tribe which are ten times the size. Together, they provide worthy subject matter for this, the first book devoted to African miniatures in the 'subtractive' mode of woodcarving (and thus differing from Margaret Plass's fine study of Ashanti goldweights, in the 'additive' mode of brass-casting). But let us return to the opening words of this introduction: the Herman collection is above all an artist's collection.

William Fagg
May 1970.

List of Illustrations

We know how irritating it is to the scholar, and how misleading it can be to the average reader, to be confronted with a reproduction say 15 inches large of an object which in reality is only three inches! We have therefore decided to use, wherever we thought it necessary, two reproductions of the same figurine, and place them in close proximity: one larger to facilitate the study of the other in actual size.

Colour Plates

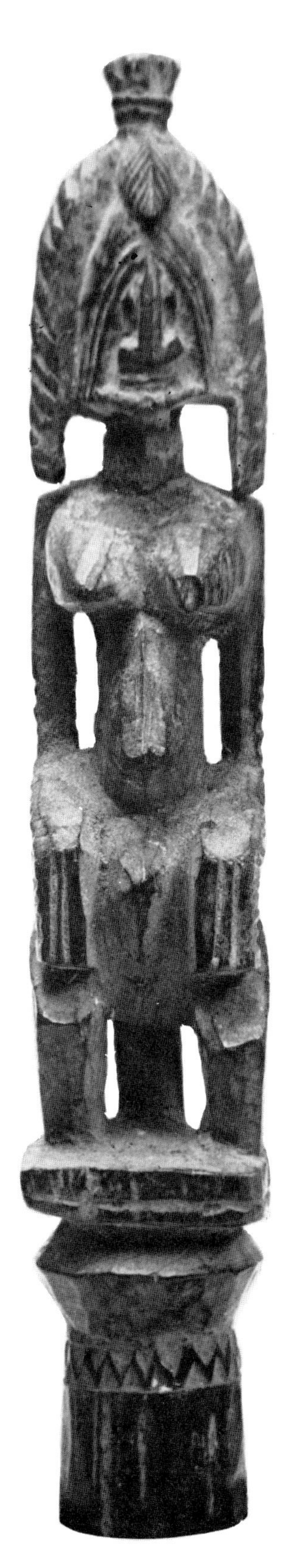

1 DOGON Staff head *5 inches*
Dogon art—which is in acute need of an unprejudiced re-examination, free from mid-twentieth-century mythology, is still alive, and is being made by Dogon blacksmiths for the people participating in the *Sigi* Festival (and sometimes, with patina added, for the export trade), even though nearly all the old art which was portable was flushed out by the scavengers of the Bamako-Paris axis some ten to twenty years ago. This tiny staff head finely illustrates one of the dominant styles of the last seventy to a hundred years, with its well-structured emphasis upon an order composed, for example, of radiating lines from the horizontal of the base of the head through some 30° to the incline of the thighs.

2 DOGON Male figure *5 inches*
This fine little figure, formerly from the André Lefèvre collection, exemplifies another and contrasting style contemporary with figure 1, but notably less structured. Its apparently shamefaced aspect is not misleading, for this kind of figure is said to represent a mythical ancestor who was guilty of contravening the incest tabu.

3 (*right*) SIENA Pair of figures, male and female *5 inches*
The Siena are the tribe which is more commonly known as Senufo; field workers report that they call themselves Siena and this therefore is the name by which they should properly be known. There is a deceptive simplicity about the carving of these delightful figures. The artist has achieved a remarkable universality inasmuch as one can imagine them as figures of one's own culture, and can almost imagine what they are doing or saying. The purpose of these figures is not known.

4 SIENA Female figure *6 inches*
This is a remarkably impressive figure, characteristic of Siena sculpture before the debasement of their style some fifteen years ago when they became primarily makers of *Kitsch* for Europeans. This one has a well marked representation of the large lock of plaited hair worn by women in the centre of the forehead, simulating a bird's beak.

5 SIENA Male figure *6 inches*
The monumentality of this sculpture is such that it would be hard to tell from photographs whether it was six inches high, or two feet, or even six feet; and in some ways the actual size might seem the least likely, so appropriate is the finish to any size. One is tempted to think that the Colossus of Rhodes may have looked something like this. The Siena used all sculptures like this in divination.

I SIENA Male figure *(see figure 5)*

6 SIENA Male figure $4\frac{1}{2}$ *inches*
This figure is attributed to the Siena, but is of somewhat aberrant style. It is a fine piece with remarkable subtleties of form.

7 SIENA Heddle pulley holder in the form of a female figure $7\frac{3}{4}$ *inches*

This carving, once more of drastic simplification, was made to hold the pulley at the top of a man's loom, from which the two heddles were suspended and alternately raised and lowered, thus creating the sheds and countersheds which are necessary in weaving. The loom used by men in western Africa produces a ribbon about four inches wide which is then made up into clothing for men.

8 SIENA Pair of figures, male and female *5 inches*

This is another variant of the central Siena style of carving, identifiable by elements of subject matter and of style. The purpose of these figures is not known, although there is a general tendency in the Western Sudan for small figures to be used in divination.

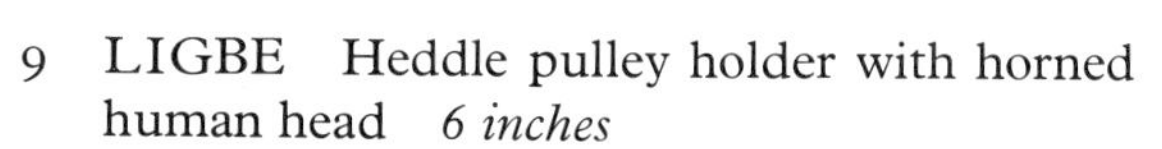

9 LIGBE Heddle pulley holder with horned human head *6 inches*

This work appears to be in the southern-most Siena or Senufo style which is practised on the fringes of Baule country by a number of small tribes including the Ligbe, Nafana, Mo, etc. The semicircular eyes with the straight line at the top are a characteristic feature of the art of this area. (*right : side view*)

10 LOBI Seated female figure *6 inches*
The Lobi or Lowiili of Upper Volta and north-western Ghana have about the simplest economy and material culture to be found in western Africa. Their ancestor figures range from sticks barely formed to suggest a human figure, to more naturalistic pieces which nevertheless are still in the nature of 'pole sculpture'. These small and doll-like carvings appear to be a recognised element in their material culture and are probably dolls to be held in the hand.

11 MOSHI Female doll *8 inches*
The Moshi are the principal tribe of Upper Volta. Their dolls provide infinite variations of the abstract human figure seen here. They do not appear to have any great symbolic significance beyond their use as girls' dolls.

12 KURUMBA Female doll *9¾ inches*
This remarkable figure appears similar to some small figures which have been found among the Kurumba in the north part of Upper Volta. The face has certain similarities to Yoruba style, but there does not appear to be any connection.

13 DAN Mask *5 inches*
The Dan-Ngere tribal complex of Liberia, Guinea and Ivory Coast is one of the most interesting in Africa but still demands much more intensive field work before we can identify the tribal affiliations of specific styles with certainty. The style generally associated with the Dan tribe is its restrained and rather naturalistic form, which is to be compared with the following piece. The piece of cloth like a mask across the upper face probably relates to the practice of painting this area in white, red and blue earth colours for ceremonies.

14 NGERE Mask *6 inches*

The Ngere form of mask is far more grotesque and less naturalistic than those associated with the Dan. As with the previous mask, it is most probable that this one was not actually made for wear in front of the face, but perhaps as a 'portrait' of a larger mask which was actually worn by the owner in dances. These two contrasting types of representation of the human face, though thought to be representative of Dan and Ngere styles respectively, appear to be sometimes found co-existing in the same village. It is curious that whereas among full-scale masks the Dan and Ngere modes are fairly evenly represented, in the miniature masks the Ngere mode is extremely rare. This piece was once in Tristan Tzara's collection.

15 GURO Heddle pulley holder
8½ inches
This heddle pulley, though almost certainly to be assigned to the Guro, is unusually ungainly for the Guro style, though it has a considerable strength to compensate for this.

16 GURO Heddle pulley holder *6½ inches*
The Guro are, or were, past masters of the art of carving heddle pulleys, and this is a classical example of the Zuenola style.

II GURO Pair of figures, male and female
7 inches
The Guro are a tribe of the Central Ivory Coast who generally are oriented towards the Baule to the south and east (although one Guro style shows rather the influence of the Bete, a group of the Dan-Ngere complex). These charming figures are in the style of Zuenola, and are more often found as superstructures to masks.

17 BAULE Heddle pulley holder in the form of a woman $7\frac{1}{4}$ *inches*
This very unusual heddle pulley could also be from one of the lesser Akan-speaking people to the south of the Baule. (*front and back views*)

18 (*left*) BAULE Pair of figures, male and female $9\frac{1}{2}$ *inches*

This is a fine example of the couple, a widespread subject in West African art which is very commonly represented in this way with the male and female figures looking slightly outwards, rather than straight forward. This always seems to convey a special serenity and self-sufficiency.

19 ALANGUA Seated female figure $7\frac{3}{4}$ *inches*

This piece is from the tribes between the Baule and the coast, and almost certainly from the Alangua. It is one of their best and most original carvings. The skilled carver's eye and hand are evident in the bold serrations of the stool (of the woman's type), which are reflected on a smaller scale in the serrations on the neck and around the face (in what may be the strap of the hat) and finally—on a larger scale again—in the cog-like hat itself. Within this framework the proportions of the body are comparable to some of the best carving of the Fang of Gaboon.

20 ASHANTI Female doll *7 inches*

Here is a more typical *akua 'ba*, as these dolls or fertility images are called by the Ashanti, except for the fact that the peripheral holes are unusually large both in size and in number. They are carried by pregnant women as charms to obtain beautiful girl babies (they are a matrilineal society), and perhaps also by younger girls who only aspire to the married state. If it is true that they were tucked into the woman's waistcloth in the small of the back, in the position in which babies are carried, this might account both for the backward tilt of the head and for its flat lenticular form.

21 ASHANTI Female doll *6½ inches*
An Ashanti group with an idiosyncratic style or possibly a related group to the south of Ashanti must have produced this piece, with its unusual proportions and the convex form of the face.

22 EWE Male figure *7 inches*

The Ewe, to whom this piece is attributed, are the neighbours of the Ashanti on the east and are linguistically related not to them but to the Fon and the Popo of Dahomey. This group of tribes are much given to the use of charms or fetishes, that is to say pieces which from the religious point of view are the lowliest of all, since they do not usually represent any individual god or even spirit but are more or less magical means of bringing the desired effect about. This does not mean, however, that they are lowly as works of art and many of them are in fact as fine as images of gods, for example some of the *nkisi* fetishes of the Bakongo.

23 FON Male figure *7 inches*

This is the Fon style of making fetishes and charms. A typical Fon head surmounts a body which is a simple tapering form like that of the ancient Greek herm. This is then bound round with a collection of wooden pins. Fetishes are used for a great variety of purposes and it is not possible to say what any given one is for, but one of their most important uses is for swearing upon.

24 YORUBA Female figure *6 inches*
The Yoruba have a broadly naturalistic form of art, but this piece is naturalistic in a special way and remarkably true to life. Evidently it shows a woman of large proportions, with plenty of fat about the shoulders, and the skirt is untidily arranged, which is most unusual. The style suggests an origin near Lagos and one is irresistibly reminded of the great market women of Lagos, who formerly wielded great power in the land. There may be some slight influence from European ideas, although probably not from European art. The function of the string is unknown.

25 *(left)* YORUBA Male figure $5\frac{1}{2}$ *inches*
This excellent little genuflecting figure, which is of unknown use, is in the style of the Falade family of Iseyin in north-western Yorubaland, where it was collected by Leon Underwood the sculptor in 1945/6.

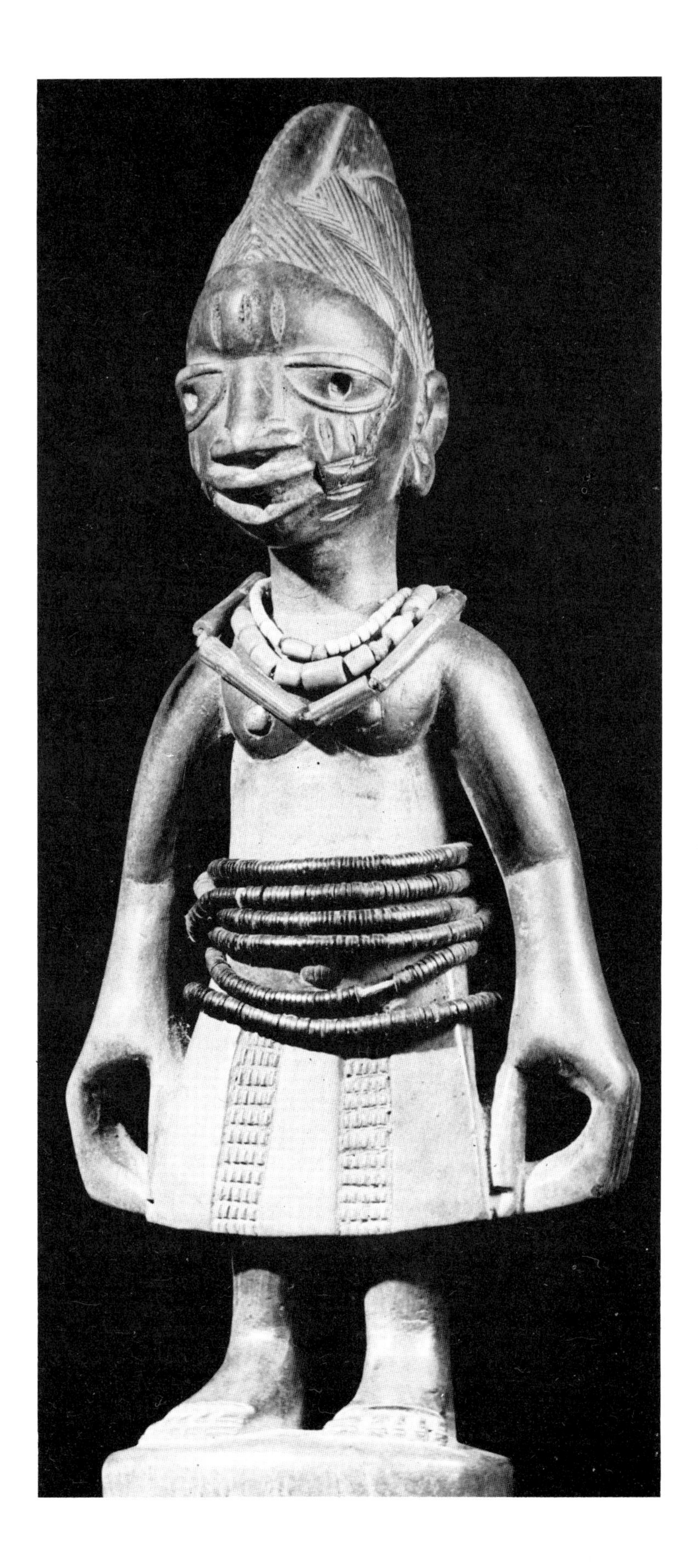

26 YORUBA Male figure $8\frac{1}{2}$ *inches*
The Yoruba, like their western neighbours the Fon and Ewe, welcome twins but regard them as the result of some kind of supernatural intervention and therefore to be hedged about with ritual. In particular, when one or both twins die, the diviner will instruct the mother to commission a carver to make either one or two figures like this, which are called *ere ibeji*. These are treated by the surviving twin or the mother as though they were the living children and are washed, 'fed', and clothed, as well as being provided with strings of beads from which the cults to which the dead child was dedicated can be deduced. This one is a fine example of the work of the Akinyode family of Abeokuta, the hands being carved large for the attachment of strings of cowrie shells.

28 (*above and right*) YORUBA Stopper with two heads $4\frac{1}{2}$ *inches*

This stopper, probably for a palm-wine vessel, may remind us of the fairly close correlation of the drinking of palm wine with the carving of wood. The area of consumption is in fact very much the same over the whole of western and central Africa. The Yoruba may well be the most enthusiastic imbibers of palm wine in all Africa. The finely carved heads appear to be in a style found a little west of centre of Yorubaland.

27 (*left*) YORUBA Female figure $3\frac{1}{2}$ *inches*

The principal marks of Yoruba style are present in the eyes and mouth as well as the facial scarifications, but nevertheless the piece is far from typical of Yoruba work and it seems likely to have originated among one of the groups on the extreme eastern boundary of the Yoruba in the former Kabba Province of Northern Nigeria. If it were a male figure, it could well have been a small piece used in Ifa divination. It might however be used in some other form of divining.

29 *(and right Plate III)* IBIBIO Mask
$5\frac{1}{2}$ inches

The Ibibio have a language and culture quite distinct from those of the Ibo, although some of their masks—those covered in skin rather than more specifically Ibibio forms such as this one—have been borrowed from them by the south-eastern Ibo. This symmetrical mask is very typical of the old Ibibio style.

30 IBO Male figure *8 inches*
The sculptor's eye can be seen at work in the alignment of the arms and abdomen and in the almost equal value allotted to each. The figure, which is of uncertain use, is from the western Ibo area near Awka, where the painful *ichi* scarification seen on the forehead is—or was—practised. This is a notably monumental figure.

31 BAGIRIMI Female figure
$7\frac{1}{4}$ inches

This piece appears to be a simplified version of the dolls collected among the Bagirimi and Kenga tribes of the Republic of Chad. The simplification, however, has served only to increase the vigour of the carving. As can be seen, the face is made with two strokes of the adze.

32 PAGAN TRIBES Female figure
8½ inches
The Pagan tribes of Northern Nigeria are typical of a form of culture which is found all along the great belt of territory from Northern Cameroon through the northerly parts of Nigeria, Dahomey, Ghana and also through Upper Volta and Mali as far as the Bambara—from whom indeed this excellent figure may alternatively originate. It appears to be the head of a staff.

33 BANGWA Male figure *$5\frac{1}{4}$ inches*
A comparison of this with figure 37 shows many subtle differences. The absence of any straight lines in the axis of the figure is another point in which they differ from those of the plains (which also invariably have a cut severing the hands from the chin).

IV BANGWA Male figure *$4\frac{1}{2}$ inches*

The Bangwa are a tribe of the Bamileke group living in the Bamenda Highlands of West Cameroon. They were among the great masters of the miniature, besides making some of the best of Africa's large sculptures. These small sculptures have a freedom of form and a marvellous exploration of movement which is found only in the grasslands of Cameroon.

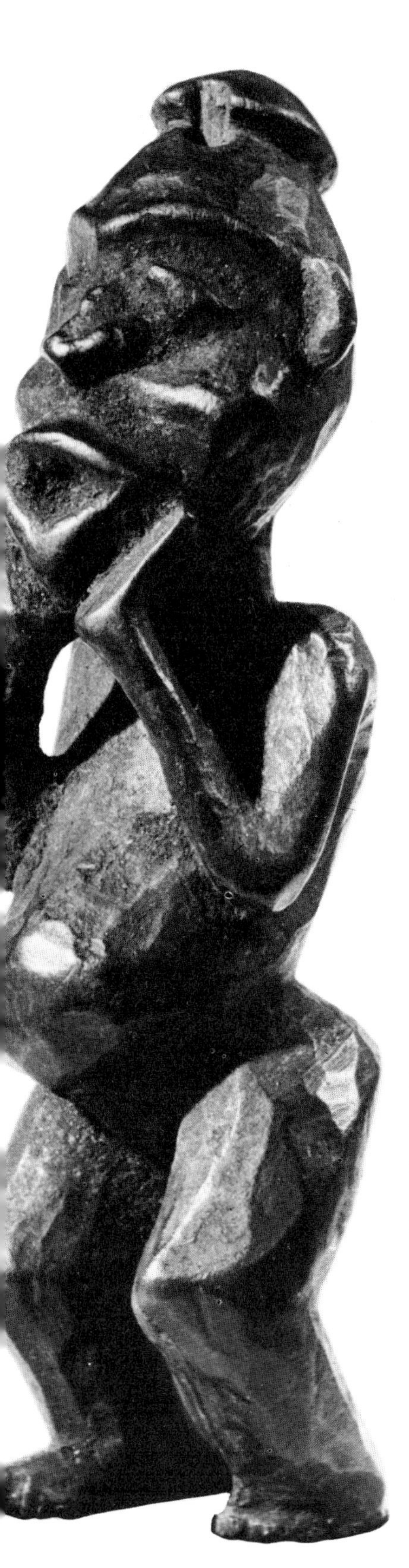

34 BANGWA Male figure
5 inches
We do not know the purpose of these figures, but the large paunch of a chief seems to occur very frequently among them.

35 BANGWA Male figure $7\frac{1}{4}$ *inches*
The unusual features of this piece may well be associated with its greater appearance of age: the acuteness of the angle between the discoid head and the neck would not be surprising if it were the oldest of our Bangwa examples. If so, it would seem that the later examples have perhaps been toned down with the passage of time, although they do not show the slightest feedback from work carried out for Europeans.

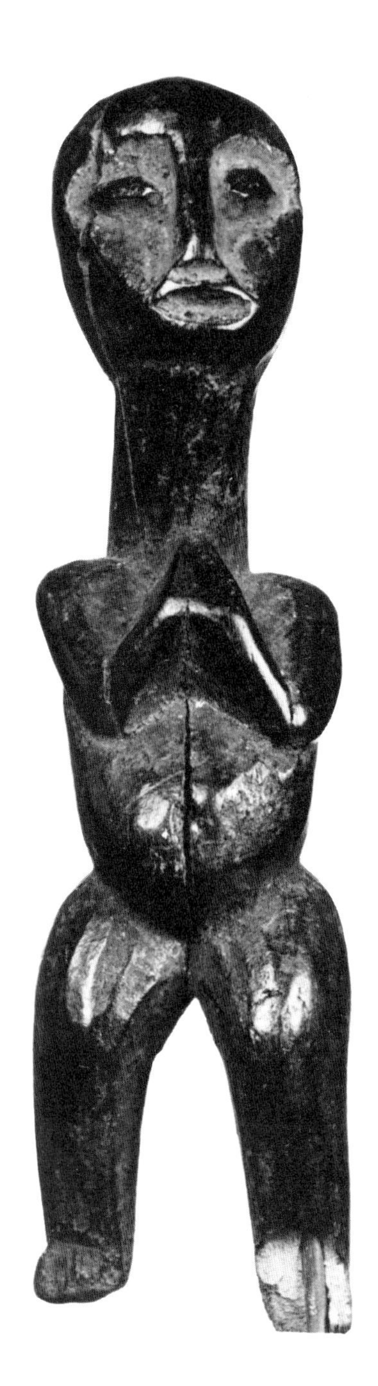

36 BANGWA Male figure $6\frac{1}{2}$ *inches*
This figure we attribute to the Bangwa from a general similarity of style, although it departs considerably from the form of the face in the piece which we have already seen. It has an admirable liveliness.

37 BANGWA Male figure *7 inches*
This form, a man with hands to chin, is evidently borrowed from tribes such as the Bafo and Bakundu of the plains to the south of the escarpment. The style, however, is totally different and in the plains version no such freedom is evident.

38 BAMILEKE Male figure *4 inches*
This may well also be from the Bangwa, but we prefer to give it the wider classification of Bamileke as it is not so typically Bangwa, although it certainly appears to have the Bamileke extravertness.

40 (*right*) FANG Female figure as fan handle *6 inches*

This delightfully simplified figure from the southern Fang, *au sexe généreux* (as the great French collector Felix Fénéon once wrote of a very much larger piece), holds an indeterminate object in the great expressionist hands. The eyes are imported nails with brass tops.

39 (*left*) FANG Male figure $9\frac{3}{4}$ *inches*

The best Fang art is remarkable for the way in which, underlying the superficial sweetness and quietism, one can often see the sculptural resolution of conflicts and opposed forces in balance. Here, for instance, the pelvic bowl (like a radio-telescope) is contrasted with the expanding forms of the upper body. On the back is an incised figure like a roughly stylized twig hanging downwards. It appears to come from the northern Fang (who call themselves Bulu), probably in southern Cameroon.

41 BAKOTA Double figure *3¼ inches*
This little charm, possibly for a twin cult, is attributed to the Bakota on account of a certain resemblance to an extremely rare large mask from this tribe, collected at Zokossoa, which is in the collection of Mrs Katherine White Reswick, now of Los Angeles (see *African Tribal Images*, 1968, No. 212).

42 NORTH-WEST CONGO Animal figure as fan handle $4\frac{1}{4}$ *inches*

This carving is unique in my experience, in being an unmistakable representation of a bushbaby. It has so naturalistic a form as to show little evidence of tribal style, but could well be from the Fang or another tribe of the Gaboon or Congo-Brazzaville, both areas where the bushbaby is found.

43 NORTH-WEST CONGO
Figure *4 inches*

The origin of this piece remains a somewhat baffling mystery. I suggest that it may come from somewhere not too far from the mouth of the Congo, possibly from Congo-Brazzaville, but possibly also from the Bayaka of Congo-Kinshasa. It appears to be a form of doll.

44 ASHIRA-BAPUNU TRIBES

Female figure $5\frac{1}{8}$ *inches*

This fine old figure is in the unmistakable style of this group of tribes, although it has been used by another tribe under the influence of the Bakongo, as can be seen by the rectangular hole excavated in the body to hold medicine. The term 'Ashira-Bapunu Tribes' is a linguistic one derived from the classification of Bantu languages by Professor Malcolm Guthrie.

45 ASHIRA-BAPUNU TRIBES Female figure
$3\frac{1}{4}$ inches

Another version of the style to which we give the name Ashira-Bapunu, but which includes also Balumbo and Mashango, shows marked differences both from the preceding and the following figure. Nevertheless, we do not yet know enough to put a single tribal name to any of the three.

46 ASHIRA-BAPUNU TRIBES
Female figure *9 inches*
The third version of this important group of styles appears to be from its southernmost extension, as it has eyes made in the Bakongo manner with pieces of glass.

V BABEMBE Male and female figures (*see figure 47*)

47 BABEMBE Male and female figures
4 inches
The Babembe are inveterate miniaturists, and only two or three larger figures are known from them. This is the most interesting Babembe work known to me. It was clearly made for use not by Babembe themselves but by a witchdoctor of the Bakongo, since this is a type of whistle used in ceremonies of witchcraft among the Bakongo, the whistle being a small duiker antelope horn threaded on string which is seen passing through the carving and out at the base. Moreover these two figures lack the almost invariable holes in the posterior for the insertion of medicine or fetish material; these are present only when Babembe carvings are to be used by Babembe themselves.

48 (*right*) BABEMBE Male figure *7 inches*
Like all the following pieces, but unlike the preceding one, this figure exhibits the characteristic body scarifications of the Babembe, all of these pieces being made for their own use. This figure seems to display a half-smiling docility, almost as if a chief were sitting for his first photograph.

49 BABEMBE Female figure $5\frac{1}{2}$ *inches*
This figure, in comparison with figure 53, though possibly a less good carving, seems to be designed to suggest a more extravert and expansive figure. Like most other carvings of the Babembe it has eyes made from small chipped pieces of European china.

50 BABEMBE Male figure $5\frac{1}{2}$ *inches*
A very different picture is presented by this sturdy example of a common Babembe subject, a man with a gun and a knife.

51 BABEMBE Male figure
4 inches
Usually, as here, the head in Babembe figures is about one quarter of the total length of the figure; often the feet are exaggerated. The trunk, however, is usually slightly longer than in nature to accommodate the elaborate scarifications used by the tribe.

52 BABEMBE Male figure
$7\frac{1}{2}$ inches
The variety of expression in these Babembe figures is remarkable. This one suggests, perhaps, an Old Testament prophet. (If I use similes from the European consciousness rather than African analogies, this is because practically nothing is recorded about these figures, which for many years were known as Sibiti figures after a village near the country in which they are found). This piece was formerly in Tristan Tzara's collection.

53 BABEMBE Female figure *$5\frac{1}{2}$ inches*
In female figures also we see a marked contrast in styles, this one being of a neat proportion and reserve, in contrast, say, to figure 49.

54 BATEKE Male figure $4\frac{1}{8}$ inches
The Bateke, who live next to the Babembe and in the immediate vicinity of Brazzaville, are famous among surrounding tribes for the supposed efficacy of their fetish figures. These are most commonly built up into a ball-like shape, with a mixture of earth and various other medicines.

55 BATEKE Female figure
7¾ inches
This is an interestingly carved figure, in which the fetish material is not so all-embracing as in figure 56. The carving of the neck may be intended to indicate goitre, which is sometimes represented in carvings in the area, possibly intended as specifics against this disease.

56 BATEKE Male figure *6½ inches*
This figure creates an astonishing effect considering that only the head is visible and even this is obscured by age and use. There are said to be two or more kinds of Bateke fetish, but unfortunately they cannot always be distinguished by internal evidence, whilst external evidence is very rarely available.

57 BATEKE Whistle in the form of a human head *4 inches*
This is a typical example of a hunter's whistle from the Bateke, who used a similar head form on ceremonial brass-plated axes. These Bateke whistles are very rare.

VI BAKONGO Female figure with child *8 inches.*

I own to a subjective feeling, as I gaze at this piece, that I could walk under the legs and that they would tower above me like the lower courses of the Eiffel Tower. It seems, in fact, to have a certain dreamlike quality, suggested perhaps by the remarkable design of the thighs, calves and feet. It probably comes from one of the inland branches of the vast Bakongo complex, perhaps in the area of Bayaka influence.

59 BAKONGO Female figure
6 inches

Congo fetishes, whether they come from the Bakongo or from the Basongye far away beyond the Bakuba to the east, occasionally have the head turned through a right-angle to the right or the left, for what reason it is unknown. This is an excellent example of the inland versions of the greater Bakongo style and may indeed be from one of the related tribes such as the Basundi or the Babwende.

58 (*left*) BAKONGO Female figure
8½ inches

This is a fetish in the strict sense, that is, a mechanism used in the control and direction of the life force for the purposes of the owner, and deriving its power not so much from the figure itself, but from the medicines applied to it by the *nganga* or witch-doctor and from the spells which he performs at the same time. The medicine on the stomach of this figure has at its centre a cowrie shell, which is usually a female symbol, and, since it is of the rarer female type, the fetish was probably intended to bring children. It is impossible to tell which is the exact front of the piece and one feels that the sculptor was constantly altering his viewpoint.

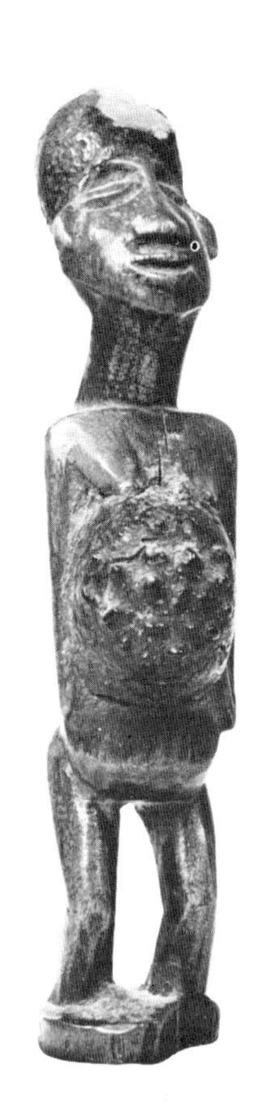

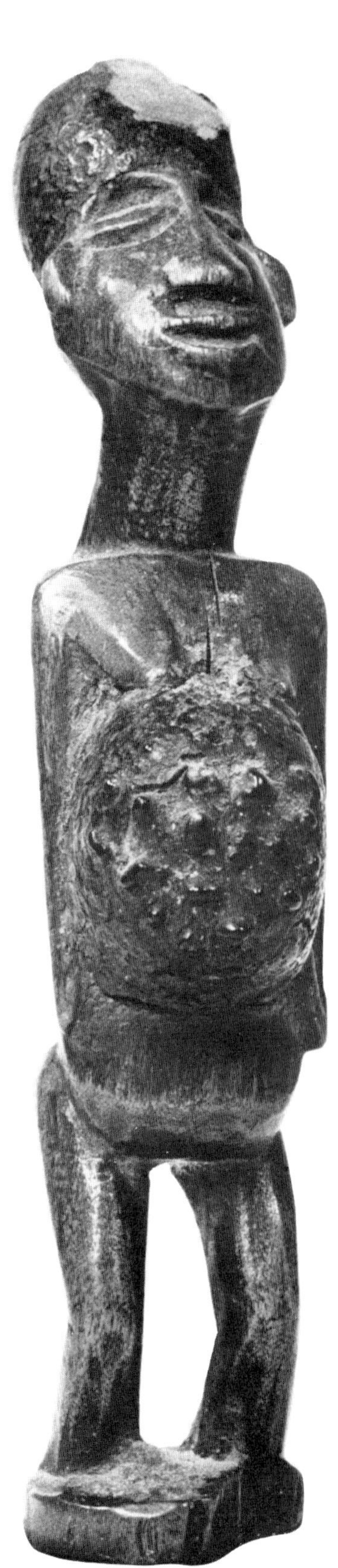

60 BAKONGO Female figure as handle *4 inches*

This tiny figure on the handle perhaps of a flywhisk is carved with an extraordinary sensuousness of line and form. The gesture of the hands placed behind the head is found especially among the Basundi and Babwende tribal groups, although the style is rather more characteristic of the Bavili on the coast.

61 BAKONGO Female figure *4 inches*

This is probably to be regarded as a figure of a woman. It appears to come from the Bavili, the northernmost coastal group of the Bakongo.

62 BAKONGO Female figure
5 inches

This expressive figure is carved in the style of the Bavili, of whom the pointed cap or head-dress appears to be characteristic.

63 BAKONGO Male figure

5¾ inches

The Bakongo are like the Yoruba in having a single great style which pervades every corner of their territory, but which allows enormous variety in treatment. This is another sub-style, nearer to the coast, and there are many more sub-styles still to come. It is a fine old carving which clearly has been much used; it is unfortunate that these so obviously functional pieces are almost never documented as to their use.

64 BAKONGO Janiform head *4 inches*
This curious carving is pierced by a slot that passes through the head transversely between the two faces and is clearly intended for a belt to be passed through it. Possibly the lower portion is meant for the attachment of some bundle or other object to be carried.

65 (*left*) BAKONGO Seated male figure
$5\frac{1}{4}$ *inches*

Here is an example, in the handle of a flywhisk, of another *genre* of art which is of great importance among the Bakongo—the figure of a European (or a Negro in European dress) who is seated upon a cask of liquor and holds a flask and some kind of drinking vessel in his hands. These carvings more than any others have fully European proportions in all except the enlarged head.

66 (*right*) BAKONGO ?Male figure *7 inches*

Here is none of the refined sensitivity which Bakongo artists so often seem to have been seeking. There is a remarkable coarseness which seems to have been entirely intentional, in the carving and the design, with its simplified legs alone balancing the head. Many such fetishes are carved with the arms stopping short at the elbow, possibly because of the expectation that they will be covered up. It is not always easy to determine the sex of Bakongo figures, for if the primary and secondary sexual characteristics have nothing to do with the purpose of the fetish they may well be left out by the carver. This piece formerly belonged to the great Danish collector, the late Carl Kjersmeier.

67 (*above and left*) BAKONGO
?Male figure $3\frac{1}{2}$ *inches*
A complete figure is presumably buried within the wrappings of this piece and one must judge it rather as a made-up object than as a human figure. As such, however, it is notably impressive.

68 BAKONGO Male figure *5 inches*
(figure only)
This axe haft, which used to belong to the late Tristan Tzara, has an unmistakable Bakongo face and head. The decorations on the body are made of pieces of wire tapped into the wood.

69 BAKONGO Male figure $4\frac{1}{2}$ *inches*
This fine little figure is by no means typical of Bakongo style, but nevertheless was probably made among them or one of the neighbouring tribes who were influenced by them. The asymmetry of the features seems intentional.

70 BAMBALA Female figure with a child
8 inches

This magnificent figure is of a type which is found among several related tribes, most notably the southern Bambala, but also western groups of the great Bapende complex, while somewhat similar figures have recently been identified among the Ovimbundu of Central Angola. It is probably an ancestor figure. At first sight, the figure looks as if it represents a sufferer from yaws, gangosa or syphilis, but statues are also subject to a similar kind of attrition though from a different cause, and here the front part of the nose has at some time been knocked off. The sharpened teeth probably indicate an actual method of filing the teeth down, which is sometimes associated with cannibalism.

71 BAYAKA Male figure
$5\frac{1}{2}$ inches

This small doll-like figure is unmistakably from the Bayaka. The circular depression for the eye orbit is in the Bayaka style, although it may ultimately be due to diffusion from the Bajokwe. The gesture of the hands, which in European terms would be indicative of submission or prayer, is widely found among the tribes of the Kwango river area.

72 BAYAKA Male and female figures *in copula* $4\frac{1}{4}$ *inches*

The union of the sexes appears to have some particular significance for the Bayaka and surrounding peoples as it often appears on their architectural carvings, though less frequently in portable art. This piece, in which a maximum degree of union is evidently achieved, may well be from the bag of tricks of a witch-doctor (*nganga*).

73 *(left)* BASUKU Male figure $9\frac{1}{2}$ *inches*
The Basuku and the Bayaka live together in the area of the Kwango and Inzia rivers. This is the characteristic Basuku form, which is occasionally, however, practised by Bayaka carvers.

74 BAYAKA Male figure $4\frac{1}{2}$ *inches*
This small figure, formerly from the collection of André Lefèvre, is clearly of the Bayaka style although the nose does not have the usual *retroussé* quality. The circular area round the eyes is a definite Bayaka feature.

75 BAJOKWE Male figure as tobacco mortar
$5\frac{3}{4}$ *inches*

Throughout a vast area of Central Africa, in southern Congo, Angola and Zambia, the styles of art have been deeply affected by the Bajokwe—a tribe of hunters who pass freely over great areas. This is their classical style of carving, and, as is often the case with artistically gifted peoples who are much on the move, they lavish a great deal of their skill on the smallest pieces such as tobacco mortars and hunters' whistles. This noble figure of a chief wears a characteristic Bajokwe head-dress.

76 BAJOKWE Male figure as whistle *4 inches*
Here a magnificent and highly original carving in the form of a tiny whistle shows a chief in a fanciful version of the royal headgear which gives the whole carving a decidedly Japanese kind of appearance.

77 BAJOKWE Whistle with human head
3½ inches
A whistle of the same type is here given a quite different form, though the process above the head is probably derived from horns of the duiker antelope as in the preceding piece.

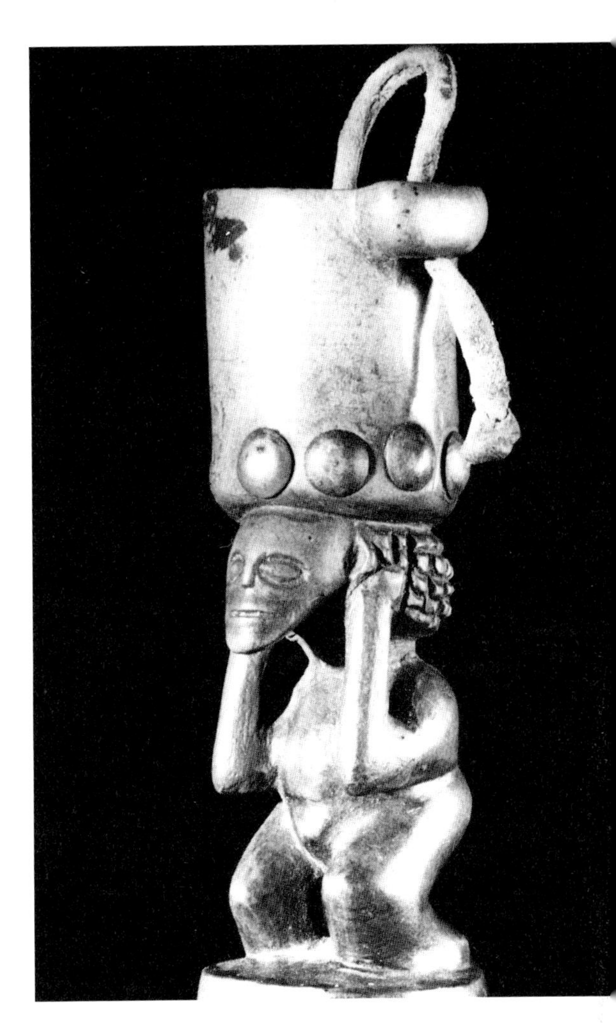

78 BAJOKWE Male figure supporting a tobacco mortar *$4\frac{1}{4}$ inches* This fine carving is certainly from the Bajokwe sphere of influence, but may be from one of the tribes in north-west Zambia, such as the Balovale, who have essentially a Bajokwe type of culture. The face is projected well forward from the main form of the cranium.

79 BAJOKWE Female figure supporting a tobacco mortar $7\frac{1}{2}$ *inches*

Bajokwe style at its most sensuous is here seen exerting an influence on the lines of the mortar. The treatment of the eyes is the most uniform element in Bajokwe style.

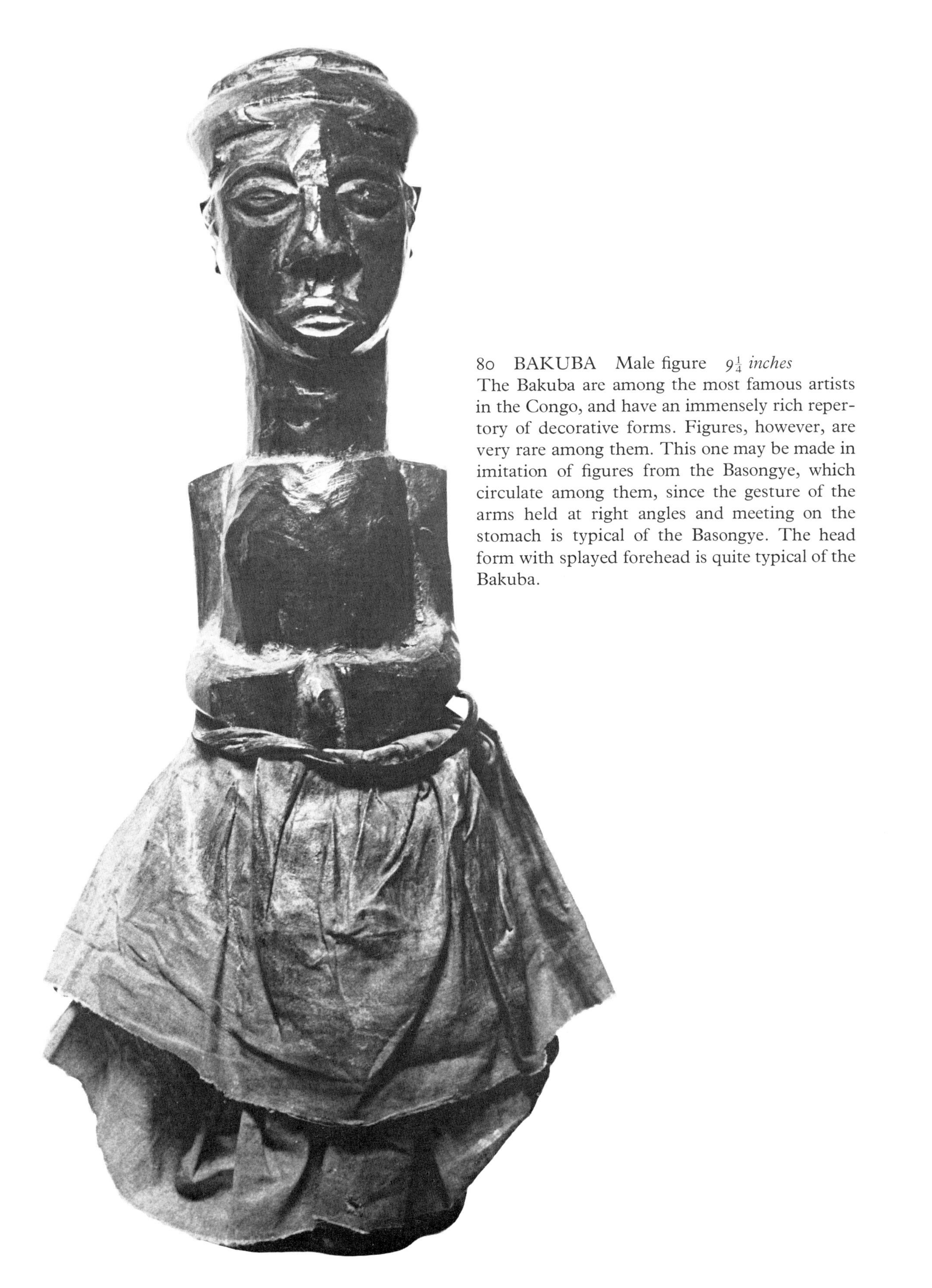

80 BAKUBA Male figure $9\frac{1}{4}$ *inches*
The Bakuba are among the most famous artists in the Congo, and have an immensely rich repertory of decorative forms. Figures, however, are very rare among them. This one may be made in imitation of figures from the Basongye, which circulate among them, since the gesture of the arms held at right angles and meeting on the stomach is typical of the Basongye. The head form with splayed forehead is quite typical of the Bakuba.

81 BAWONGO Carrying hook with human head $4\frac{1}{4}$ *inches*

This carving is somewhat tentatively assigned to the Bawongo, an autonomous group culturally, but not politically, affiliated to the Bakuba. The method of use is to tie a bundle to the hook by means of the flanges at the base and then to hang the hook on the hut wall or on the belt.

82 BALWALWA Male figure *6 inches*
I have tentatively assigned this very interesting cubistic figure to the Balwalwa because the strange form of the nose recalls the male masks of this tribe which have an exceptionally salient nose. This tribe—though close neighbours of the Bajokwe—do not show any influence from them and in this they are almost unique.

84 BENA LULUA Male figure *$3\frac{3}{4}$ inches*
This is also a readily distinguishable Bena Lulua piece, although very different from the last. It appears to be one of the figures called *lupfingu*, according to Himmelheber, which were provided with a small receptacle in which offerings of kaolin are made.

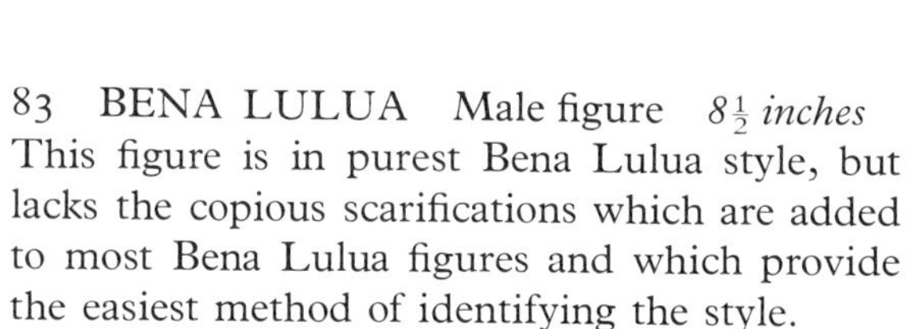

83 BENA LULUA Male figure *$8\frac{1}{2}$ inches*
This figure is in purest Bena Lulua style, but lacks the copious scarifications which are added to most Bena Lulua figures and which provide the easiest method of identifying the style.

85 BENA LULUA Squatting male figure *3½ inches*
The elbows-to-knees position is particularly characteristic of the Bena Lulua. It recurs in widely separated parts of the world, as in New Guinea. It has been conjectured that the foetal position is represented.

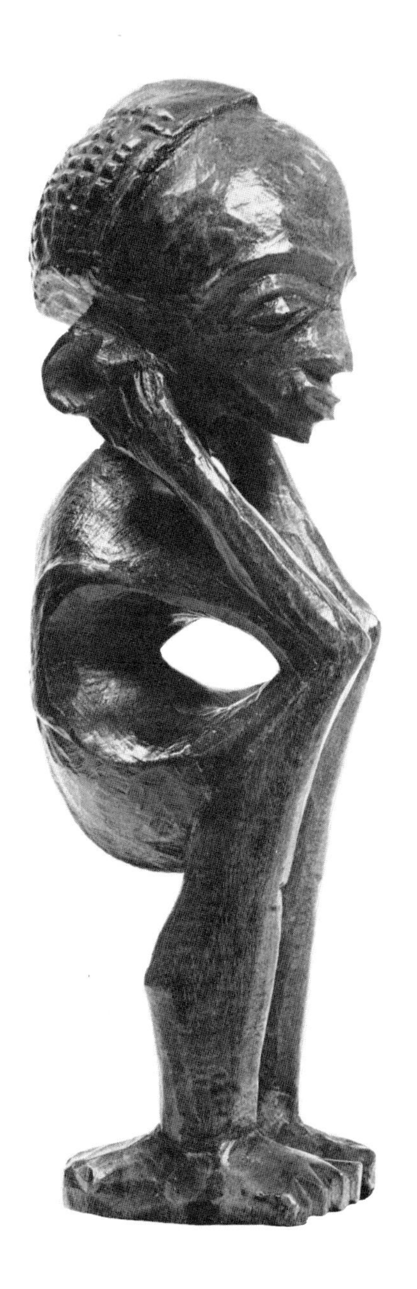

86 BENA LULUA Female figure *6 inches*
This is a classic version of the squatting female figure. The face is typical of many of the larger figures made in the 1880s or earlier.

87 BENA LULUA Male figure supporting a tobacco mortar *5 inches*

This mortar is very similar to some made by the Bajokwe, but the body is very much of the Bena Lulua technique and the elbows-to-knees position also supports this attribution. A well-worn pestle is present and shows the manner in which the mortars were used in preparing snuff.

88 BALUBA Divining implement with human head
4 inches

Divination provides many of the miniature carvings of the Baluba. This implement, sometimes called *katatora*, is provided with a hole large enough to accommodate the index finger of the diviner himself and the person consulting him. They move the object back and forth upon an oiled wooden surface, while intoning the names of the possible culprits, etc. Eventually the object sticks and the culprit is found. This one and figure 89 are probably from the central Baluba.

VII BALUBA Divination implement with human head (*see figure 89*)

89 BALUBA Divination implement with human head $5\frac{1}{2}$ *inches*

Here is another example of the *katatora*. This one has an unusually masterful face, showing some slight resemblance, probably accidental, to the masks of the Balwalwa.

90 BALUBA Female figure $6\frac{3}{4}$ *inches*

This curious figure is from the area of Kamina among the Shankadi sub-tribe of the Baluba. It used to belong to the sculptor, Leon Underwood, and is of great interest for the manner in which the limbs are represented in relief on the long cylindrical body.

91 BASONGYE Male figure *5 inches*
This is an example of an old carving, with a duiker horn to contain the magic substances.

VIII BASONGYE Male figure
3 inches

The Basongye are famous among the surrounding tribes for the manufacture of fetishes in the strict sense of machines for controlling life force, as are the Bakongo. This one is typical of the style, although overlaid with some red earth or powdered cam wood. The fetish material is mostly placed in the top of the head, where an iron nail is its principal ingredient.

92 BASONGYE Male figure *5 inches*
This is a slightly more modern version than figure 93, with home-made Basongye brass nails used to embellish the carving.

93 BASONGYE Male figure 8 inches
This figure, though seriously eroded, is an excellent work. The duiker horn is present, as frequently, in the head.

94 BASONGYE Male figure *7 inches*
This fine piece may possibly be from the neighbouring Batetela, but is most probably from the Basongye, as the elements present are mostly typical of the style, although the treatment of the lower aspect of the head is sometimes found amongst the Batetela.

95 BASONGYE Male figure *5 inches*
Here there is strong influence from the Baluba, but the square jaw and the position of the hands suggest that it should be placed among the Basongye. As no breasts are shown, it is assumed to represent a man with a large belly.

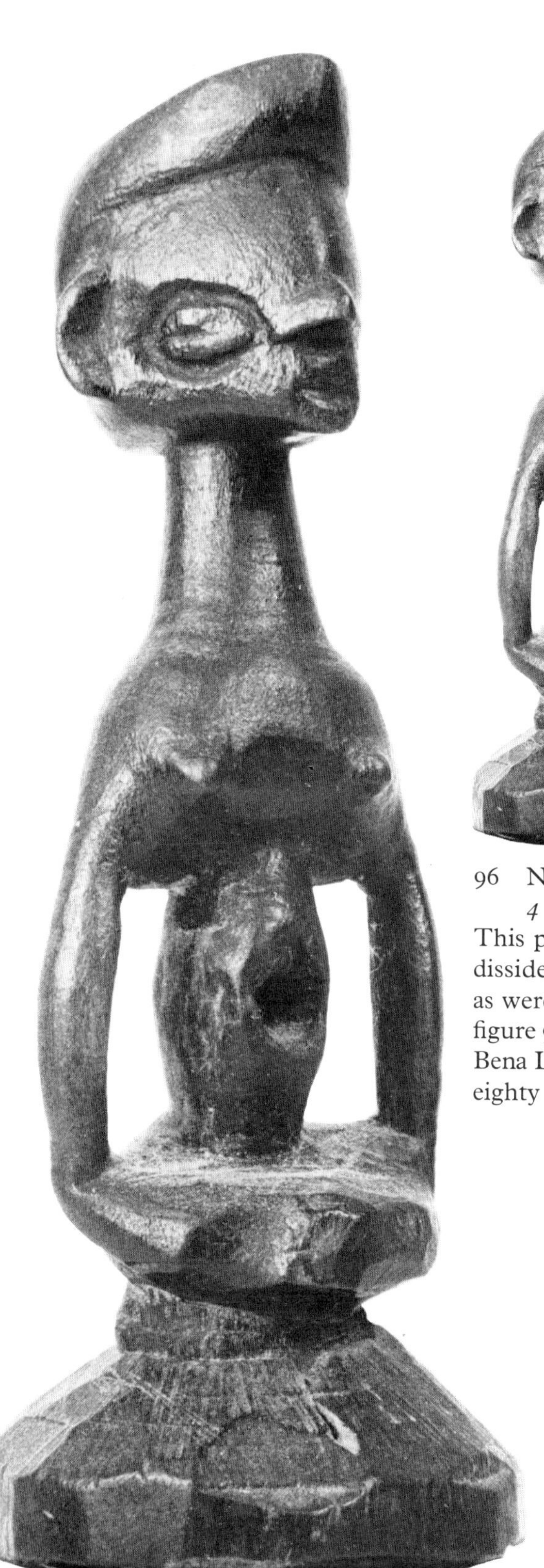

96 NSAPO-NSAPO Female figure
4 inches
This piece was collected from the villages of the dissident tribe of Basongye around Luluabourg, as were figures 97 and 98. This style, and that of figure 98, may perhaps have originated among the Bena Lulua, and been differentiated over the past eighty or ninety years.

97 BASONGYE Male figure *6 inches*
This work, in pure Basongye style, was collected by Timmermans among the Nsapo-Nsapo, who are of course a Basongye offshoot, although mixed with elements from other tribes.

98 NSAPO-NSAPO Kneeling male figure *5 inches*
This, and figure 96, are examples of a style peculiar to the Nsapo-Nsapo, and apparently owing little to their Basongye origins.

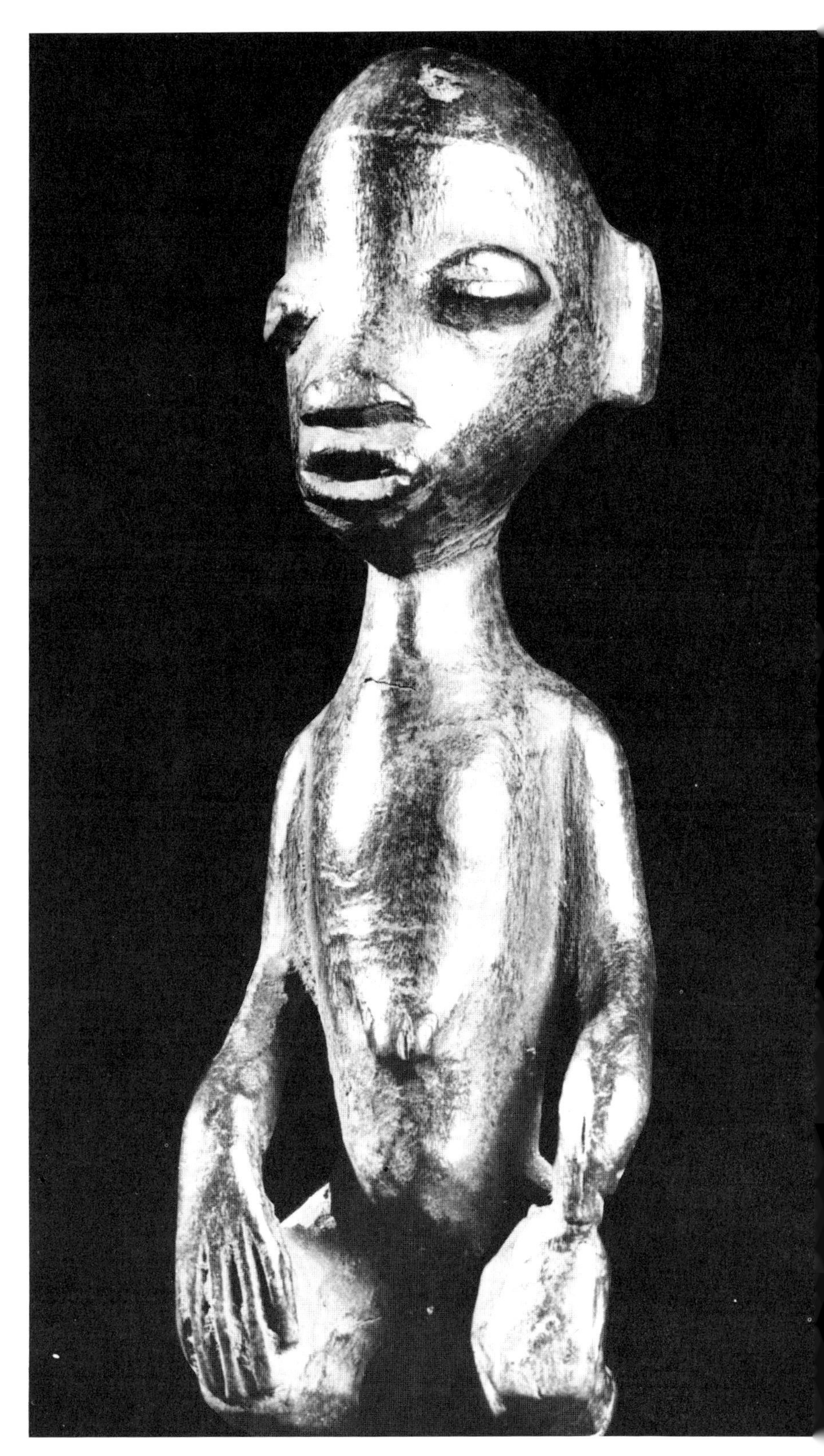

99 *(above and right)* BALEGA
Janiform figure $5\frac{1}{4}$ *inches*
This figure, collected among Balega by Nicolas de Kun, is an example of the works made for the Bwame Society which exerted all power among the Balega tribe, and used works of art as mnemonics and symbols in inculcating the rules of tribal life in the course of the progress of the people through several grades of the society. There is seldom much difference shown between the sexes and it cannot be said whether this represents a male or female, or both in one. Wooden figures are said to be valued even more highly by the Balega than ivories, which are much commoner.

100 UBANGI Female figure with rattle
9 inches
This marvellous evocation of the dance—in which it may well have been used—may be regarded as 'pole sculpture', but nevertheless achieves great subtlety in the sinuosity of its forms. The Ubangi-Shari area seems perhaps the likeliest for its place of origin.

101 MAKONDE Stopper with human head *3 inches*

The Makonde, who live near the east coast of Africa on the borders of Tanzania and Mozambique, are the last of a chain of peoples who practise a rather similar art and span the area between the Great Lakes and the sea. The Yao, at the western end of this area, are in touch with the Baluba or Baluba-influenced tribes of Zambia and Malawi. The Makonde also appear to show some Baluba influence in their larger works. Their exquisite bottle-stoppers foreshadowed the tourist art which replaced them some thirty or forty years ago, and which now rivals that of the Akamba in volume (and exceeds it in variety).

102 ZULU Female figure *8½ inches*
The Zulu do not practise much wood carving apart from staff heads but, when they do, it is usually interesting and on occasions as sophisticated as any African artists' sculpture. This work is in a style in which several much larger figures are known.

BIBLIOGRAPHY

WILLIAM FAGG *Tribes and Form in African Art*, London 1966, and Boston; *The Art of Western Africa* and *The Art of Central Africa*, London 1967, and New York

WILLIAM FAGG AND MARGARET PLASS *African Sculpture: An Anthology* (revised edition), London 1970, and New York

MICHEL LEIRIS AND JAQUELINE DELANGE *African Art*, London 1968, and New York

ELSY LEUZINGER *Africa: the Art of the Negro Peoples*, London 1960, and New York

DENISE PAULME *African Sculpture*, London 1962, and New York

MARGARET TROWELL *Classical African Sculpture*, London 1964

LEON UNDERWOOD *Bronzes of West Africa*, London 1949; *Figures in Wood of West Africa*, London 1964; *Masks of West Africa*, London 1964